Little Pearls

Little Pearls

Margaret Malloy

First published in 2011 by
Margaret Malloy

© Copyright 2011
Margaret Malloy

The right of I Margaret Malloy to be identified as the author of this work has been asserted by her in accordance with the Copyright, Designs and Patents Act 1988.

All Rights Reserved
No reproduction, copy or transmission of this publication may be made without written permission. No paragraph of this publication may be reproduced, copied or transmitted save with the written permission or in accordance with the provisions of the Copyright Act 1956 (as amended).

Printed and bound in Great Britain by:
Proprint, Remus House, Coltsfoot Drive,
Woodston Peterborough PE2 9JX

To
the friends
of the Scottish Christian
Writers Association
and to the special people
of the Helensburgh Writers group.
Finally, to Fred - for his past
friendship and most
inspiring words.
Thank you.

Foreword

Little Pearls is a collection of spiritual poems, meditations and songs that have been compiled throughout the working years of the author.

Ms Margaret Malloy who is originally from Dumbarton, worked professionally as a nurse in Glasgow, Greenock, then Bridge of Weir, until retiring to the rural district of Cove, near Helensburgh.

The poems, although they have been written with a, certain simplicity are embellished with little nuggets of inspired wisdom and are not without the ability to challenge the Christian, as well as comfort when the spirit has ebbed.

Contents

His Lullaby	1
To Know Him	2
The Vision	4
Genesis	6
Provision	7
The Delay	8
Little Joys	10
Photograph	11
The Watcher	13
The Burden	16
Dependability	18
The Sectarian	20
The Holy Place	21
Fragile Force	22
Photograph	23
Hope	24
Memories	26
The Enemy	28
The Fear	30
Photograph	32
Wonderment	33
Song Of Love	34
Unconsoled	35
Fellowship	36
Libra	38
Song Of The Valley	39
Glory	41

Going Home 43
Photograph 45
The Crowns 46
Song Of Praise 50

His Lullaby

*Down from His glory He came.
Down from a glorious reign.
Leaving a kingdom above,
Jesus the Shepherd of love
and that we might understand
how our salvation was planned
born in a manger was He
and He did all this; for me.*

*Room in a manger, alone,
where my redeemer was born.
Mary; the mother He knew,
wrapped Him in mantle of blue
and that we might understand
how our salvation was planned,
born in a manger was He
and He did all this; for me.*

*One day, they led Him away
for He a debt had to pay.
Now; from His kingdom above,
Jesus is reigning in love.
And that we might understand,
how our salvation was planned,
born in a manger was He
and He did all this; for me.*

Music – Mozart (lieder)

To Know Him

A little child of six of so,
a childish mind that sought to know,
with influence and time to grow,
began to learn about Him.

And as the knowledge grew with age,
revealed within the printed page,
I ventured to another stage
of wanting to know of Him.

Treading doctrinal avenues,
no thought deprived – no lack of views,
from Greek to Gentile, on to Jews,
I studied hard to know Him.

Sadly, alas, alluring charms
drew innocence with open arms.
I craved the pleasure that disarms
the mind, from thinking of Him.

Ah! But, although the garish way
disclosed its talent to betray,
it proved a blessing, in a way,
for now; I longed to find Him.

Such emptiness I soon discerned
and sorrow from my sin, I learned,
was bleak, intense, and justly earned
these days I lived without Him.

Oh how I wish I could express
the bliss that charged my consciousness,
the night I knelt and prayed 'Lord;
bless or blame; just let me find You.'

Then silence! Broken, only by
my mumbled pleading – to atone,
and sensing I was not alone,
I wept with shame before Him.

My spirit's ear, alone, can claim
that, 'come to me! I'll take your pain.
Through searching, there is much to gain
but you must yield; to know me.'

Although my eyes, no form could see,
His presence breathed reality
and all my guilt dissolved when He
at last, brought me; to know Him.

The Vision

There is a vision – just ahead,
 that I have long beheld.
it is the frame of one who walks
by Christ Himself, compelled.

Now; walking slowly, for the road
is difficult – so hard
the light, although the light is Christ,
by selfishness is marred.

He's tried to comfort, yes; I know,
with words, just meant for me
but I have been so dull and slow,
though seeing – never see.

His promises, so often given
so very lightly heard
I'm hunting to the gates of Heaven
for yet – another word.

*But since He made me rest awhile
within my calling place,
it wasn't just to humble me
or put me in disgrace.*

*He set me down beyond all aid
except His arm divine,
that I might learn to trust alone
His mighty hand in mine.*

*To learn to trust when faith is balanced
by a single thread
and all seems quite impossible
(this way that I am led).*

*So, trusting Him, I'll rise again
to heights I never knew,
to know each word He speaks is mine
and every promise true.*

Genesis

(From out of nothing - He created . . .

Novas expand an atom source;
The sea swells from one blotted mark.
The fire's inferno flames its force
from just, one solitary spark.

Such tiny flakes of woolly white,
that melt, upon the fingernail,
can raise, then plunge, with awesome might,
the blast that wrecks the sleepy vale.

And, little shoots of limpid jade,
through time, maturing, tier on tier,
expand beyond their cradle glade
to pierce the shrouded troposphere.

A microscopic zygote swells
to subdivide and grow its own
unique, maturing body cells
of tissue, fluid, blood and bone.

And, newborn beams, they spread
prismatic particles – of every shade.
Oh genesis; it must be said,
your world is wonderfully made.

Provision

I gave a pound or two away
to someone with a lack
but, in a while – it's nice to say
I found it coming back.

For when that need was met
though with a cost – if truth be told
an unexpected tax rebate
returned it double fold.

It made me think! If I was blessed
with wealth enough – would I
grasp luxury or choose some
tiny mouths to satisfy?

For Lord; it's Your profound desire
for those who gain success
(from out of Your vast treasury)
to succour those with less.

But then, it takes a special trust
with gifted wealth or fame
to keep the heart from planting
tempting roots of greedy gain.

So: when You say You'll meet my need
whatever – great or small,
just make me grateful and content
with anything at all.

The Delay

**Called to follow – time for change,
unskilled, but with a keen desire,
every tripping step attempted
served to flame faiths little fire,
 and; what seemed impossible to me;
at times, did amply prove
as God swept away the obstacles
and left me free to move.**

I expected, then, to have success
with such a trusted guide,
that I very proudly walked,
my flag unfurled – against the tide.

**You can picture the bewilderment
that wrestled with my pride
when it came as such a blow to find
my final steps denied.
Many mixed emotions mingled
mentally, as I became
quite convinced that I must choose
another path – another aim.**

Nagging doubts, then, claimed success
although I still clung to my guide
but my feet began to drag,
 my ensign – trailing in the tide.

Disappointment grasped despondency
as I made to depart
but the wheels of change,
that should have turned,
held fast: they failed to start.
So: I thought perhaps to quit
the venture now may seem unjust
for God's little signals, still
gave some encouragement to trust.

Well; it came as such relief to find
it was just a delay
while I learned a painful
(yet essential) lesson for the way.

'Child; you know
I never promised you success,
to see this through,
all I ever asked was faithfulness,
no matter what; from you.
So, don't covet gain or glory
as the world may crave, your role
is to trust my guidance; win or lose,
to ascertain my goal.'

So: I claimed my Lord's priority
when self-importance died,
for I scrambled up the rock
and tossed my ensign; to the tide.

Little Joys

A summer's evening;
with a hint of breeze upon my face.
A cuddled nest of feather-down
and four small beaks in place.

A tiny bird – caught by the cat
soon in my hand it lies
and after resting for a while,
released – it upward flies.

Large, clustered blooms of tinted pink
surround my parking place,
and first, out of my hanging basket,
peeps a pansy face.

A brand new carpet, thick and freshly
laid in perfect style,
supports neglected shoes
as toes repose on woolly pile.

The smell from the upholstery
inside my brand new car
or bathe in steamy clouds of scented
bubbles from a jar.

*A 'run to cuddle' greeting
from a little child I love.
To find a dress I really like,
still fits me like a glove.*

*A feral kitten, drenched and cold,
when coaxed at last to creep
so slowly – underneath my arm
and purr itself to sleep.*

*To lift the phone and hear a voice
I haven't heard in years
or watch a shooting star
that all too quickly disappears.*

*An unexpected answered prayer
which lifts my mood of grey,
a red bibbed robin near my chair
that wouldn't fly away.*

*It's nice recalling little joys
drawn from my memory store
and if I live expectantly
I'll find so many more.*

The Watcher

The moon bathed dark Gethsemane
as silence fell around
and shaded mist of evening fell
to kiss the dusty ground.
The birds – they had already gone
it was as though they knew
that someone would be there
the whole night through.

The yellow moon shone brighter still
as though it tried to see
the silhouettes of sleeping men,
now, outlined there, for me
and as the beams pierced through the trees,
another I could trace,
as sobs were heard
ascending from that place.

'Oh Father could there be another way?
I fear the man made cross
Oh tell me of some other way.'
And as He prayed in agony
He slightly turned His brow
to show the drops of sweat
were bleeding now.

*As on time passed – the weeping frame
was all that I could hear.
I watched as if my pounding heart
would reach His listening ear.
Another seemed to join Him there
and hold His bleeding head
yet – still, He raised His eyes to Heaven-
and said;*

*'Oh Father could there be another way?
I fear the man made cross
Oh tell me of some other way.'
And as He prayed in agony
He slightly turned at will
to show the drops of sweat
were bleeding still.*

***Then, presently, a sound came through
that I could barely hear.
It seemed like some unearthly power
or someone He held dear.
And as they talked and reasoned why
the awful day must be
was when He turned His head
and looked – at me.***

*'Oh Father could there be another way?'
He feared the man made cross
He pleaded for some other way.
Serenely then – He rose to go
He knew the reason why . . .
and as He walked away
He smiled – goodbye.*

The Burden

*A friend of mine has problems
laced with troubles – and although
I've given sound support, they still
cling, unresolved – and so . . .*

*My spirit, like a leaded bubble,
tumbled in despair,
then spattered into nothingness,
my vein attempts at prayer.*

*I tried to think of something else
to stem the ache inside
but, back it creeps then splashes
like an evanescent tide.*

*If I could just – some trust apply
for – faith is what I lack,
sometimes I tiptoe out to try
but then, come running back.*

*And so – with every route explored
I come again to say,
'Oh please, will you take over Lord?
resolve, in any way.'*

*'Child; in your tender innocence,
endeavouring to care . . .
without my guiding influence,
may prove – too much to bear.*

*But, love – should it prevail
must harbour trust . . .
 which, now you lack,
for when you gave the cares to Me,
 you, promptly, took them back.*

*I have already planned ahead
in answer to your plea.
Just work through as My plan unfolds,
the burdens – leave with me.'*

Dependability

*There's a godly call to follow
but some dear ones they may say,
'Don't commit yourself too deeply,
leave tomorrow – come and stay.'
Here; you'll find attractive choices
where your spirit can aspire
to sincerely serve your master
with that flame of ardent fire.
But again He comes; this master
with His 'Child; come follow me.'
Should you rise, to meet the challenge,
keep dependability.*

*Those we love if somewhat distant
may deny God's guided choice.
Oh, they like the change within you,
hear the glory in their voice,
but when dawns the cost . . . the challenge,
understanding leaves the floor
and with cutting disapproval,
mentally they bar the door.
Well my friend; the years have taught,
some disappointments have to be.
Shed that long-desired acceptance
keep dependability.*

*But, you know; time marks the changes
in a 'soul maturing' sense,
for your constancy of heart
will reap his promised recompense.
And when having such assurance
that your God is in command
of this awkward situation,
they will come to understand.
For it's true; the years have taught
God honours those who faithfully
stand through thick or thin; whatever,
with dependability.*

The Sectarian

*I've witnessed that prejudiced demon begin
to kindle your hate – when determined to win.*

*You wave self-control, as you master the fray
and woe-betide any who get in your way.*

*I'd like to consider friend; how would you stand
if suddenly beamed to that Heavenly land?*

*Supplied with a mansion and having to share
with those you despise, and you think won't be there.*

*Perhaps you would tolerate turnstiles to guide
each group to their place to maintain that divide.*

*What triggered this motion? What rooted then grew
this partisan madness: Who influenced you?*

*This cavalier attitude; could it imply
you guess your endeavours are blessed from on high?*

*I know I would find it so hard to relate
or trust to a god who gives sanction to hate.*

*So: why can't you practice His 'far-better part?'
for, nothing can bar a true worshiping heart.*

*No pushy religion – no loss – creed or state,
no government law – nor your dominant hate.*

*So friend; just remember, when planning this role
to master your brother, love; conquers the soul.*

The Holy Place

*Only a woven veil conceals
our God's 'Most Holy Place' of prayer.
Only His perfect sacrifice
reveals the way to enter there.*

*There, where Jehovah never slumbers
keeping us, surely, in His sight.
There, where He soothes the saddest soul
with sounds of singing – in the night.*

*So! Don't give ear to cruel deception
falsely declaring that you must,
before you enter – fiercely strive
to shed sin's parasitic dust.*

*Nor should overt, or screened emotions
stirring unworthiness or shame
keep you from God's profound desire
to grant His child a 'Holy Name.'*

*So; through that veil – come; boldly enter.
Leave all regrets – your sandals too.
Come through that bloodstain on the lintel,
where God – He waits, my friend – for you.*

Hebrews Ch 10 - V19

Fragile Force

*What destiny
imprints this drive
to quit a dank, Moroccan shore
and gamble such a tiny life
with fragile wings of gossamer.
That frail – unflinching, little force,
to grace the bracing, polar sky
must scale the granite peaks- then pass
dark tangled woods and pencil pines
to land the Knapweed's tufted eye
in clover grass.
But, since her offspring, yet unborn
must feast – the thistle – to survive
she'll wait the wind to steer her course,
then soar the deep – where sail-boats writhe
and plummet – swirling seas of brass.
She'll travel – till she's
'home and dry'
that
butterfly.*

Hope
(Sure And Certain)

Hope can be barren, when void of fulfillment
just longing for something we wish could be sure
and when prolonged it gives rise to impatience,
there's nothing else for it, we wait; we endure.

Fortune may smile, we encounter the excellent
Then, there's the dice with its possible part.
Too many dreams offer casual chances –
but, can we know certainty, right from the start?

Friend; in your obvious longing for clarity,
there are some things about hope you should know.
It needs an atom of trust – in a promise
before it's desired expectation can grow.

It doesn't spring from a lucky encounter,
acquiring consent in a moment of chance,
nor does it pamper to sentimentality,
day-dreamy heads in a cloud of romance.

This hope makes our tiny spasms of panic,
that jar – momentarily, fade in God's light,
making us braver and much more determined
to claim his 'for certain' instead of 'it might.'

It strengthens when it confronts tribulation,
confirming its ground with endurance until
all we desire, or expect from his covenant,
patience will reap, as we wait on His will.

So; sooner or later, (it may be much later)
just perish the thought that 'perhaps it will be.'
If God has promised, there must be no doubting,
But, stay ever faithful my friend, wait, you'll see.'

Memories

Time at last to contemplate
Retirement; with its severed ties.
Thoughts of winning, losing failing,
some regrets I realise.
For some foolish acts of madness
jar my mind to force a few
painful flashes causing sadness,

memories of blue.

So! I bring them, spread before Him
can I hear my Saviour say?
'Child; the sins have been forgiven
when you told Me on that day.'

But although I know I told Him
there persists this sense of blame
spreading like a smoky smouldering
to re-ignite the shame.
All that arrogance and wounding
yes; and I remember too,
giving little help or comfort,

memories of blue.

Once again, I spread before Him
and, again hear words I know.
'Child; those sins have been forgiven
you must learn to let them go.'

Could I ban the searing flashes,
or retrace – with empathy.
Trade those heated rages with some ashes of humility.
All that arrogance and wounding,
ah; but I remember too
when you came, my Lord; and eased my

memories of blue.

You disclosed my trend to store the guilt
and so discretely shelve;
for I gained immense relief
when I – at last – forgave myself.

The Enemy

Some people say they believe in a God
but the Devil is only a blind
and; it's been said that this sin is self-will
for most folks are inherently kind.
How many people will swear on 'The Word'
then select cosy parts to believe!
Well: diluting the pure is his favourite lure
for that devil delights to deceive,
Oh yes!
The devil delights to deceive.

As the prince of this world,
this was no satisfaction
for he would have taken the sky
and established his throne in Jehovah's domain,
thinking, he could be as the Most High.
He promises bliss, then; with wonders of darkness
entraps with a dancing delight,
but still, there are those who will not be convinced
for he comes as an angel of light
Oh yes!
He shines as an angel of light.

He hinders our God's little rootlets of reason
by snatching the seed as it's sewn.
He slanders and martyrs the saints by inflaming
those blind 'silly minds' of his own.
It's true there are times when God's children are tried
and it's then that they need to be strong,
but if in their plight, they hold out for the right,
by resisting, they'll find he has gone.
Oh yes!
They'll find their accuser has gone.

But wait! There's a glorious anthem resounding,
a victor's triumphant refrain,
for there came a Lord who defied death's intention
and rose from that devil's domain.
Now gone is the guilt and the power of death
that the evil one gripped in his palm.
For now; there is freedom for all, who, by faith
are redeemed by the blood of the Lamb.
Oh yes!
Redeemed, by the blood of the Lamb.

The Fear

My loving Lord
I have this nagging fear plaguing my soul.
I've tried to drive it out by reason,
still it has control.
It came upon me suddenly
to force this grim review
and plummeting depressions depths,
I lost my sense of You.

This fear of loneliness and pain
That war and hate can bring
To know the chains, the force, the blade,
man's hostile reveling.

My flitting thoughts tried, like a moth,
to settle on some light,
like martyrs with such radiant joy
who yield, to win the fight.
Or Peter, who in dread denied
his dearest friend and yet
that cruel demise (to glorify his Lord)
he bravely met.

If I could face the 'what might be'
without this nagging pest,
behead the dreaded demon
and let courage brave the rest.'

*'My child; Man's evil way may render
darkness to the soul,
but it must pass the brightness
of my presence – to control,
But even if it permeates the faith
 that you have known,
I'll never, ever, let you face
uncertainty alone.'*

*Oh yes; my grace will meet what comes,
not – what might never be.
Hold fast to how we faced the past,
tomorrow; leave with me.'*

Wonderment

What stirs this timeless mystery?
When little sprigs of withered wood
which, lie, so cold, inanimate
and make me think they never could
begin, just when the time is right,
to stir from their hard, earthy mound
and pierce such tender little points
of silken white through granite ground.

Song Of Love

There's no perfect love
but from my Lord.
No perfect love – so wondrous – so divine.
He charmed my heart.
Lily of my soul – tender and precious
Precious, Lord to me.
On wings of perfect love I fly,
uplifted high – beyond my sinful brow.
Forgiven now!
Jesus, his own blood supplying,
was there such a need for dying?
Gave Himself in love to set me free.
Oh perfect love – every moment free,
flowing now, to me,
flowing to me,
from Calvary.
Blest Calvary.

Tune – Etude Opus 10 no 3
(Tristesse – sadness)

Unconsoled

Freeze the dawn!
Go; trap the sunshine
where no pinpoint can survive,
split all laughter from its joy –
erase that smile.
Hiss the breath out of its sac
till only death remains alive,
ban Gilead's balm – let nothing reconcile.
Pass that pat of muted kindness,
shrink the cords of love's resolve,
neither cause again their bonds to interlace.
Let no mind of change – whatever,
ease the ache nor blame absolve
till I wallow – just a while –
in grief's embrace.

Fellowship

*Bless the day when we will worship
all together – in the Lord.
Not in separated circles,
drawing those with one accord.
I have searched for God's perfection
for so many claim 'the True'
each sincerely dedicated
with their practiced points of view.*

*Pondering those varied doctrines
made my choice what seemed the best.
Left aside what very likely
could upset my cosy nest.
But, my lord, with patience travelled
on my proud, judgmental trip,
till I grasped the Spirit's teaching
of His boundless fellowship.*

***Time disclosed the wider scene
as, slowly, I became aware
that no group could prove perfection
yet; His own shine everywhere.
For the Lord with His discernment
said, 'You know, you limit me
child, I do not dwell in buildings
but in hearts – redeemed and free.'***

*Freedom now from Man's opinion!
Sweet assurance Lord – I know
I can worship with the blessed
    anywhere I go.*

Libra Days

*The verdant flora fades – to yield its glory to the brown
and stubble fields are bathed in mist as furrows slowly drown.
Cracked, shriveled leaves go gusting up to dart the drift
below and morning's low maturing sun – reflects a copper
glow upon the town.*

*It features perfect rounds of coated silage – every bale
tight bound in glossy black and stacked upon the distant dale
and on the hill, the lambs, no longer lambs, for they have grown
to emulate the ewes, now mute, detached – but not for long
for 'tups in field!'*

*In spring, our robin may endure his speckled sons but with
their outward flight – he now defends his province to the death
and through the fallow field some swallows swoop then skim
the spires
to score a farewell melody by landing on the wires
and then; they're gone.*

*And little ardent bees caress each blossom's nectar site
to leave their tiny legacy and germinate delight.
For there's the honey – jams and rainbow fruits, now sealed;
and more,
all labeled, with the cider-jars that pack the pantry floor
beside the wines.*

*But now; the air is chilled and with that early dusk – the pale
mist, now thick like teaseled cotton, permeates the dale.
The sun? he's gone with gold; but left the ripened sky ablaze
with quilts of rose – for nature paints her most amazing art,
to close
her Libra day.*

The Valley

Courage, Dear One; don't you falter,
though the way is dark as night,
there's a friend who'll never alter
his resolve to guide aright.
Don't let simple trust desert you
when emotion would betray.
Keep on bravely, sad or weary
till the day . . .
when the sorrow that is pressing,
it will pass, then you will know
that He only led His daughter
    through the valley.

Courage, Dear One, don't give up,
though dark persistence reaps despair
and you long to rise and soar
the wind of change – to breathe its air
but, the God who knows you well,
so quick to bless and never blame,
has an ache, so deep within Him
at your pain.
Courage Child you, soon will sense
the reasons why He planned it so,
why He had to lead His daughter . . .
    through the valley.

See ahead, a glorious dawning
shining skies of blue above.
Look before you – look around you
glorious with His wondrous love.
Jadeite pastures – fresh as springtime,
little blossoms fill the air
with a perfume just for sharing
as you tarry there.
Freely then – you'll trust your Saviour
Freely then – you'll see and know
that He only led His daughter . . .

    through the valley.

Glory

Lord; what will I find in Your glory?
with martyrs, disciples and kings,
all sitting around in Your presence
and sharing, such high, wondrous things.

How awesome to listen with reverence
what many there present will tell
of great mighty acts they've accomplished
for You, who has loved them so well.

I feel I have little to offer
from 'out of the best' I have known.
I've only accomplished the simple,
such weak little seeds I have sown.

So; what will I find in Your Heaven?
although I will love being there,
redeemed – yet, the least of Your children
with no mighty deeds to declare.

*And yet – I have seen – there are actions
in life that are destined to last,
when you waved a banner to honour
our humble attempts of the past.*

*For, I can recall tiny ripples
that spread, far beyond mortal eye
or seeing my molehill of effort
expanding and peak to the sky.*

*And, goals with their grand aspirations,
they now have a chance to excel
for you germinate all we offer,
to spread – just how far? Who can tell.*

*So' now, as I ponder Your Heaven
with martyrs, disciples and kings
all sitting around in Your presence
and sharing such high wondrous things.*

*I'll listen with reverence, of stories
but also, my Saviour, I'll tell
just what You have helped me accomplish,
because You have loved me; so well.*

Going Home

*Taking
the arbour path . . .
He came;
seeking me out,
my brave earth angel.
Of late – this golden oak
had grown gaunt,
like a lean - grey – twig.
Sucking breath to energize
his staggering gait
he sat – close,
exhaling weariness.*

*I prayed
for words,
He wanted none!
Softly – sharing
the 'heydays'
of his mercurial youth,
his memory – then,
oh so gently – danced me
through the delights
of his sweetheart days.
But something in his eyes
implied . . .
while dancing down
that treasured past,
'we've danced
the last.'*

I prayed
for healing.
He wanted none!
His destiny was carved out
by 'that good man the Carpenter'
who was oh; so gently
easing him towards
God's celestial door,
now, slightly ajar.

And then,
he left!
Straining to capture his
fading foot fall silent,
my stemmed emotions, burst . . .
such a reservoir of tears,
for I felt I had given him no gift,
but I still taste that glorious feast
he set before me
that day he came down . . .
the arbour
path.

The Incorruptible Crown

*There's a crown to be won,
when you run the strait race
like the Grecian athletes of old.
It means – strict discipline
and a spiritual striving,
consistently eager and bold.
Being temperate,
with a true - holy ambition
and seeing the line further down,
you must give – all you've got, of your best'
when contending
for God's*

Incorruptible Crown.

The Crown Of Life

There's a crown to be won
by the faithful and brave
who are tempted and tried to the last.
They take all the worst of the evil one's best
when their colours are nailed to the mast
and for those who possess
a true love of the Lord,
they rejoice as the martyrs proclaim,

'Jesus is worthy!

For His is the power
that nerved us
as we
overcame.'

The Crown Of Righteousness

*There's a crown to be won
by the faithful
who eagerly preach the 'good-news'
of the Lord.
Their goal is to harvest the saints of tomorrow
by sowing the seeds of the Word.
And what will it be for the Saviour's beloved
as they long for their Lord to appear?
Well – this glorious crown will be theirs
when the sky is alive with the cry –*

'He is here.'

Crown of Glory

There's a Glorious Crown to be won
    By the elders
    who nourish the lambs
    in their care.

Their love is expressed with a
    Holy devotion,
their counsel, consistently fair.
They shoulder the weak
and encourage the stronger
defending their flock – till the day

When the Chief Shepherd returns,

    For His own

With their crowns - that shall not
fade away.

Song of Praise

*Come on my poor sinking heart
come and give to the Lord
the many blessings that are due.
Praise him for His grace and His favour,
all my journey through.*

*In the night – in the day
any season – come what may,
there will always be cause to sing.
So: come on, let it go
and let the rafters know
He's king,
come on and sing –*

*My Lord will love me forever
My Lord will love me forever
My Lord will love me for evermore.*